For my parents, Angie and Patsy Pepe, who let me be me —MP

*For my parents, Vic and Kay Streufert,
who encouraged me with love —JLSP*

*To the baseball fans in my life, past and present:
Pop, Dad, Drew, and Henry —SG*

About This Book

The illustrations for this book were done in digital gouache. This book was edited by Christy Ottaviano and designed by Tracy Shaw. The production was supervised by Patricia Alvarado, and the production editors were Marisa Finkelstein and Jen Graham. The text was set in Albert Sans, and the display type was hand-lettered by Mary Kate McDevitt.

Text copyright © 2026 by Maria Pepe and Jean L. S. Patrick • Illustrations copyright © 2026 by Sarah Green • Cover illustration copyright © 2026 by Sarah Green • Cover design by Tracy Shaw • Cover copyright © 2026 by Hachette Book Group, Inc. Photo credits: pages 42, 43 top, 44, and 45 bottom: Courtesy of the Maria Pepe collection; page 43 bottom: Courtesy of the Newark Public Library; page 45 top: Courtesy of Catherine Berdanier • Hachette Book Group supports the right to free expression and the value of copyright. The purpose of copyright is to encourage writers and artists to produce the creative works that enrich our culture. • The scanning, uploading, and distribution of this book without permission is a theft of the author's intellectual property. If you would like permission to use material from the book (other than for review purposes), please contact permissions@hbgusa.com. Thank you for your support of the author's rights. • Christy Ottaviano Books Hachette Book Group • 1290 Avenue of the Americas, New York, NY 10104 • Visit us at LBYR.com • First Edition: March 2026 Christy Ottaviano Books is an imprint of Little, Brown and Company • The Christy Ottaviano Books name and logo are registered trademarks of Hachette Book Group, Inc. • The publisher is not responsible for websites (or their content) that are not owned by the publisher. • Little, Brown and Company books may be purchased in bulk for business, educational, or promotional use. For information, please contact your local bookseller or the Hachette Book Group Special Markets Department at special.markets@hbgusa.com. • Library of Congress Cataloging-in-Publication Data • Names: Pepe, Maria, author. | Patrick, Jean L. S., author. | Green, Sarah, illustrator. Title: The girl who changed little league : the true story of Maria Pepe and her battle to play ball / by Maria Pepe and Jean L. S. Patrick ; Illustrated by Sarah Green. • Description: First edition. | New York, NY : Little, Brown and Company, [2026] | Summary: "A picture book biography that tells the story of Maria Pepe, the eleven-year-old girl who changed the course of Little League history forever." —Provided by publisher. • Identifiers: LCCN 2024048450 | ISBN 9780316464239 (hardcover) • Subjects: LCSH: Pepe, Maria—Juvenile literature. | Little League Baseball—History—Juvenile literature. | Women baseball players—New Jersey—Biography—Juvenile literature. | Baseball players—New Jersey—Biography—Juvenile literature. | Discrimination in sports—United States—Juvenile literature. | Baseball for women—New Jersey—Juvenile literature. | Classification: LCC GV865.P447 A3 2026 | DDC 796.357092 [B]—dc23/eng/20250127 • LC record available at https://lccn.loc.gov/2024048450 • ISBN 978-0-316-46423-9 • PRINTED IN DONGGUAN, CHINA • APS 10/25 • 10 9 8 7 6 5 4 3 2 1

THE GIRL WHO CHANGED LITTLE LEAGUE

The True Story of Maria Pepe
and Her Battle to Play Ball

By **Maria Pepe** &
Jean L. S. Patrick

Illustrated by
Sarah Green

Christy Ottaviano Books

LITTLE, BROWN AND COMPANY
New York   Boston

Every day after school, Maria finished her homework, grabbed her glove, and sprinted down seven flights of stairs to play ball.

Stickball.

Slapball.

Wiffle ball.

BASEBALL!

Maria Pepe loved baseball best of all.

She cheered for the Yankees, traded cards with her friends, and asked for baseball equipment each year on her birthday.

The more she played, the better she got.

Hitting, *pitching,*

catching, sliding.

But there were no sports teams for girls in her town of Hoboken, New Jersey. And when it came to Little League—girls were not allowed.

In the spring of 1972, when Maria was eleven years old, a new Little League team started in Hoboken. Maria's friends, who were boys, walked to the corner to sign up for tryouts.

Maria followed along. But when she got to the building, she only peeked inside.

"**Why aren't you coming in?**" asked Coach Jimmy.
"**I'm a girl . . . ,**" she said. "**But I can play ball.**"
"**Well, what are you waiting for?**"

Tryouts were held near the old sewage plant. The air stunk, and the ball skipped off the pebbles on the infield.

Maria played as well as the boys. Even better.

And when it came to pitching, Maria excelled.

After the second day of tryouts, Coach Jimmy read the names of those who had made the team. **"Louie . . . Nicky . . . Maria!"**

The Hoboken Little League season began with a parade. All the teams and coaches marched down the street by the Hudson River.

Maria felt like she had hit a home run.

There she was—the only girl in a Little League uniform.
Gray with yellow letters.
Gold stirrups over her socks.
And a cap that fit just right.

At the first game, Maria ran onto the field. The fences sparkled. White chalk baselines stretched their arms to welcome her.

Play ball!

Opposing players jeered: **"Two, four, six, eight. Pitcher's got a bellyache!"**
Maria's teammates cheered: **"Come on, Maria. You got this!"**
Maria wound up and fired the pitch.

Strike one!

And when the game was over, guess whose team scored the most runs?

At the third game, Maria pitched again.
Reporters stared. Parents griped. Coaches complained.
"Wait till headquarters hears about this!" shouted one of the coaches.
"I just want to play ball," Maria said to Coach Jimmy.

Soon enough, the men at Little League headquarters in South Williamsport, Pennsylvania, heard about Maria. They contacted the Hoboken Little League and informed them they were in danger of losing their Little League charter.

Maria sat in her living room with her mom and dad as Coach Jimmy explained.

If Maria continued to play, ALL the teams in Hoboken would lose support from Little League. No insurance. No uniforms. No umpires.

Maria didn't have a choice. She would have to be removed from the team. The hardest part was giving back her uniform.

Maria ran to her bedroom and sobbed. Who were these men at headquarters? Didn't they care about her ability? She hugged her cap and glove.
She just wanted to play the game.

Meanwhile, a group of strong, smart women heard the news. They belonged to an organization that helped women who were treated unfairly. They called Maria's parents and talked for a long time. Would Maria and her parents allow them to take her case to court?

"Let them," said Maria.

Her parents agreed. **"We have to try."** Maria wouldn't be present in the courtroom, the women later explained. But she would get lots of attention. Would Maria have the strength to be brave?

The complaint against Little League was filed. News traveled fast. Even the New York Yankees heard about Maria.

Maria cheered up when they invited her family to a baseball game against the Detroit Tigers. They sat in box seats!

Next, she was a guest on a famous morning television show.

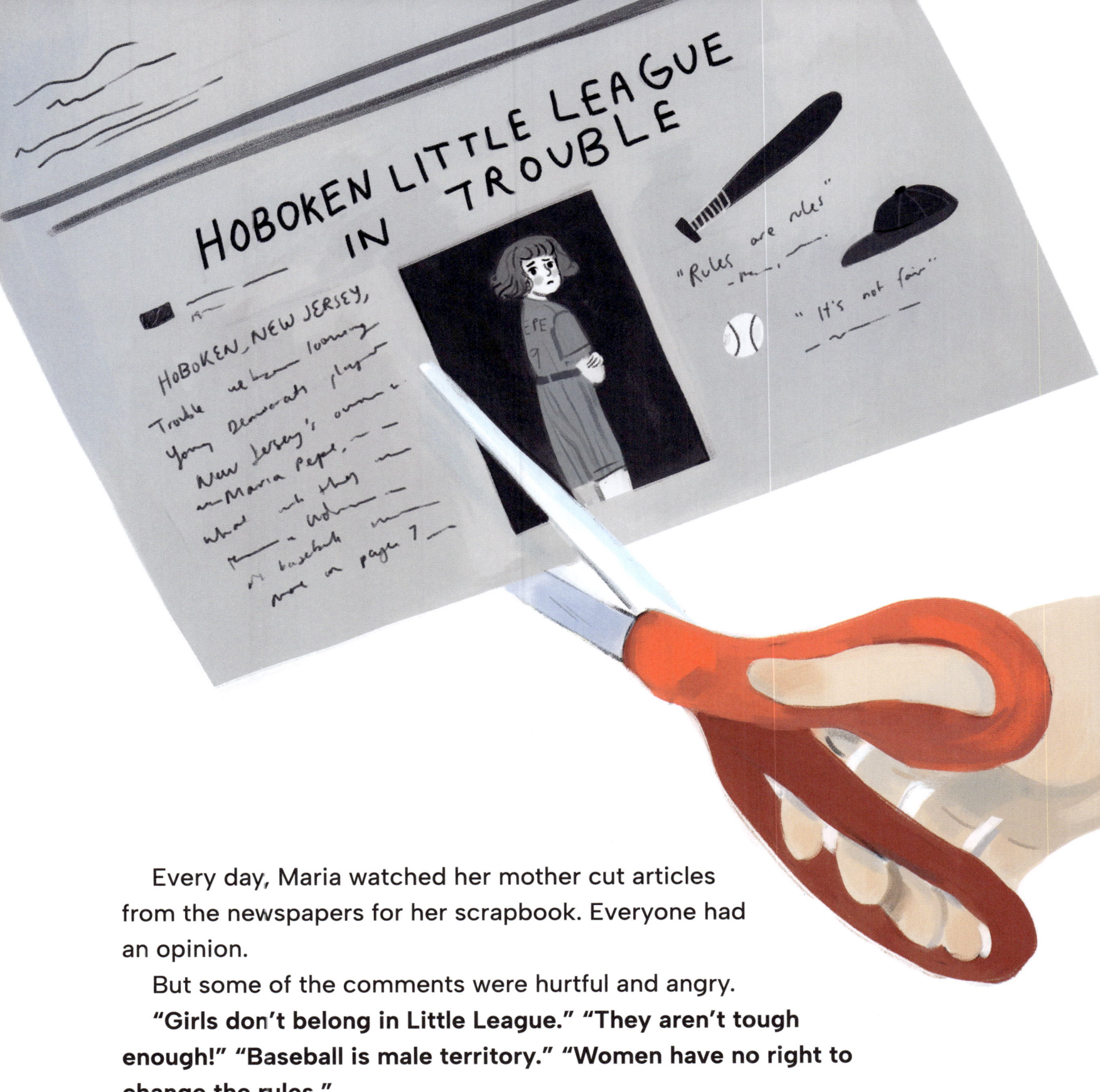

Every day, Maria watched her mother cut articles from the newspapers for her scrapbook. Everyone had an opinion.

But some of the comments were hurtful and angry.

"Girls don't belong in Little League." "They aren't tough enough!" "Baseball is male territory." "Women have no right to change the rules."

Why were people so upset?

The attention on Maria grew.
Reporters followed her everywhere. Cameras, too.
One of Maria's friends wasn't allowed to play with her anymore.
"Sorry, Maria," he said. **"My mom is worried about your wanting to play ball. She doesn't want me to be involved."**

And sometimes, it was scary. Once, when she rode alone in the elevator of her apartment building, a man pointed at her.
"Why are you causing all this trouble?" he yelled. **"Girls should be at home with their mothers!"**

Day after day, Maria stayed brave.
She just wanted to be back on the ball field.

The summer passed.

Then another summer.

Maria read, rode her bike, and shot hoops at a nearby park. She loved going to the Jersey Shore with her family, far away from the attention.

In the fall of 1973, Maria's case finally went before the New Jersey Division on Civil Rights.

The experts for Little League argued that girls SHOULD NOT be allowed to play.

Little League has always been for boys.
Girls might get hurt. Their bones are weaker.
Little League teaches boys about citizenship and sportsmanship.
Boys should play with boys. Girls should play with girls.

The experts on Maria's side argued that girls SHOULD be allowed to play.
> Girls need the same opportunities as boys.
> Girls at this age are often bigger than boys. Their bones are often stronger.
> It's good for girls to learn about citizenship and sportsmanship.
> Boys and girls must learn to play and compete together to succeed in life.

They had one more important reason, too.
> The baseball fields are public property.
> They are for everyone—including girls!

On November 7, 1973, hearing officer Sylvia Pressler announced her decision. Girls must be allowed to participate in Little League.

"**The institution of Little League is as American as the hot dog and apple pie,**" she stated. "**There's no reason why that part of Americana should be withheld from girls.**"

After school that afternoon, Maria flew up the seven flights of stairs to her apartment and opened the door.

"You won!" shouted her mother.

Maria's heart leaped. She dropped her book bag and marched through the living room, celebrating with every step.

But deep down, she knew the painful truth.

She was thirteen years old now—too old to play in Little League.

That evening, Maria's father wrapped his strong arms around her.

"I won't get to play," whispered Maria.

"Just think of all the girls who *will* get to play," he answered. **"It's because of you, Maria. You opened the door!"**

The battle wasn't over. Two thousand Little League teams threatened to cancel their seasons if girls took the field. But on March 29, 1974, New Jersey's Superior Court upheld the ruling. **Girls must have the opportunity to play.**

The decision had a far-reaching impact. Brave girls from other states also fought to play.

And guess what? On June 12, 1974, Little League changed its rules. Across the country, girls joined the boys, pitching and hitting and sliding and catching—all playing the game of baseball.

As for Maria's cap and glove? They found a place, too.

Note from Maria Pepe

My personal experience with discrimination at such a young age did not deter me from playing sports. In fact, it made playing sports a large part of my life. In high school, I played four years of women's varsity basketball, and at Saint Peter's College, I played four years of women's varsity softball. From there, I competed for twenty years in recreational softball leagues. Participating in sports helped me both professionally and personally to appreciate the importance of teamwork, winning and losing, and so much more. These are the values that Little League has as its mission.

In 2004, for the thirtieth anniversary of the New Jersey Superior Court's ruling, Little League honored me with an invitation to throw out the first pitch at the Little League World Series in South Williamsport, Pennsylvania. Meeting Dr. Creighton J. Hale (the president of Little League during the court cases) and shaking hands with him was a healing moment. Especially when he shared that his granddaughter played ball.

The World of Little League Museum asked for my original glove and baseball cap. Later, my Little League baseball cap was transferred to the National Baseball Hall of Fame and Museum in Cooperstown, New York, where it became part of their *Diamond Dreams* exhibition about the history of women in baseball.

One of my most meaningful experiences

Maria in uniform, playing for the Hoboken Young Democrats Little League team, in May 1972.

was being asked to give a testimonial speech to judges and lawyers at the sixtieth anniversary of the New Jersey Law Against Discrimination. I fought back tears as I thanked them for defending the rights of girls to participate in Little League Baseball. At the event, I also received a plaque with a powerful message: "You have established a strong legacy and have provided an excellent example for others to follow. Continue in your mission . . . to protect and defend the rights of others."

It took years to understand all the emotions I felt about being in the national spotlight at such a young age, especially being involved in a controversy. Some have left good memories, and some have left tough ones. I still remember when my mother handed me the scrapbook of the Little League articles and court documents when I was in college. I knew that one day I would write about my experience. As I reflect, I realize this book isn't just about baseball, but about the changing views of girls' roles in playing sports and in society in general.

Little League batting cage dedication in Hoboken, New Jersey, on April 16, 2016.

It has been over fifty years since I stepped onto the pitcher's mound in Hoboken and the 1974 court ruling that followed, and I have come full circle. I still live in Hoboken, where the batting cages at the Little League field are named after me. Currently, I dedicate my time and support to encouraging girls to follow their passions and believe in themselves. The best part of all is the privilege of watching girls play baseball and participate in the sport I love.

I will always be extremely humbled by and grateful for the unwavering support of my parents and the National Organization for Women. Thanks also to my coach, James Farina—I will never forget those three games I did get to play. I'd also like to thank Baseball for All, New York Girls Baseball, and Little League for their support of girls' baseball today. And special thanks to my coauthor, Jean L. S. Patrick, without whom I would not have been able to create this book. I hope my story is both educational and an inspiration to children to believe in their abilities and to do what they love.

Maria in uniform, looking from the dugout, in May 1972.

Girls in Baseball: Yesterday and Today

Women have been part of baseball for more than one hundred years. Early heroes include Lizzie Arlington, Jackie Mitchell, Toni Stone, and the members of the All-American Girls Professional Baseball League.

In 1984, Victoria Roche of Belgium became the first girl to play in the Little League Baseball World Series. As of 2024, twenty-three girls from all over the world—including the United States, Canada, Guam, Germany, Belgium, Japan, Russia, Saudi Arabia, the Czech Republic, and Australia—have played in the Little League Baseball World Series.

Currently, an estimated 100,000 girls are playing youth baseball, often on boys' teams. However, Baseball for All offers girls' teams the opportunity for national competition. Young women may also participate in Major League Baseball's Breakthrough Series, try out for USA Baseball's Women's National Team, and compete in the Women's Baseball World Cup.

Beyond Baseball

The impact of Maria's victory stretches beyond baseball. When Little League opened its doors to girls in 1974, it immediately began to sponsor Little League Softball (perhaps to steer girls away from playing baseball). Little League Softball continues to be popular and has its own World Series.

Maria also brought national attention to the importance of providing girls with the same opportunities as boys. In the process, she helped change society's attitudes about the roles of girls and women.

Maria and Title IX

In June 1972, Congress passed Title IX, allowing girls to have the same educational opportunities as boys. But Title IX didn't allow Maria to play in Little League. Why not? The laws surrounding Title IX were still being written. Also, Little League did not receive federal funding.

However, some legal scholars believe that the battles and victories of female athletes (including Maria) during the early 1970s influenced lawmakers to include sports as an essential part of Title IX.

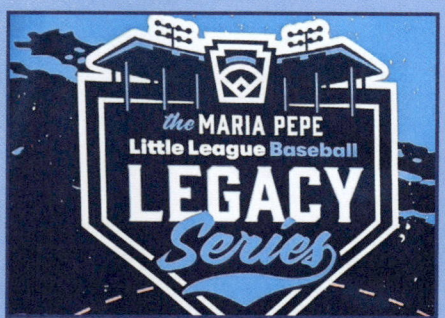

Logo for the Maria Pepe Little League Baseball Legacy Series in June 2024.

A Fifty-Year Milestone

In June 2024, Little League celebrated fifty years of the inclusion of girls with the Maria Pepe Little League Baseball Legacy Series in South Williamsport, Pennsylvania. Girls from thirty states and provinces participated. "It was one of the best experiences of my life," said Maria. The event was part of Little League's continued effort to provide equal opportunities for girls.

Little League also honored Maria's legacy by officially enshrining her into the Hall of Excellence, the highest honor Little League bestows.

Note from Jean L. S. Patrick

When I was growing up in the Chicago area, I spent my summers on the bleachers, watching my brothers play Little League Baseball. It didn't matter that I played better than most of the boys. Because I was a girl, I was not allowed to join them. When I was eleven years old, a neighbor showed me a newspaper clipping about Maria. I couldn't believe her courage!

As an adult, I gathered my own courage and sent Maria an email. A friendship formed. And little by little, she shared her precious story, as well as deep emotions from her two-year battle with Little League. As Maria's story touches the world again, I hope you will be inspired to be brave and to include others, both on and off the field. Many thanks to agent Alexandra Penfold, editor Christy Ottaviano, and the team at Little, Brown Books for Young Readers for believing in the importance of this story.

Maria with coauthor Jean L. S. Patrick at the Maria Pepe Little League Baseball Legacy Series on June 8, 2024.

Note from Dr. Judith Weis, National Organization for Women

Judith Weis with Maria at National Girls & Women in Sports Day, sponsored by New Jersey City University, on January 29, 2017.

The Little League case was a highlight of my years with the Essex County chapter of the National Organization for Women, a nationwide women's rights organization. As chapter president, I was familiar with the New Jersey civil rights law. When I read in the newspaper that the Hoboken team had to kick Maria out because she was a girl, despite being an excellent player important to the team, I realized that they had violated the "public accommodations" section of the law, since games were played on public property. We filed charges to the New Jersey Division on Civil Rights. When we won the case, the hearing officer said that Little League was as "American as . . . apple pie" and there was no valid reason to exclude girls. I am very proud to have been a part of this history-making case.